CHAPTER & *verse*

1000 YEARS OF ENGLISH LITERATURE

CHRIS FLETCHER

THE BRITISH LIBRARY

Charles d'Orléans in the Tower of London (see page 10).

Published on the occasion of the exhibition 'Chapter & Verse: 1000 Years of English Literature' in the Pearson Gallery at The British Library, London, supported by Pearson.

PEARSON

ISBN 0 7123 4671 6

First published 2000 by The British Library, 96 Euston Road, London NW1 2DB

Designed by Julie Rimmer

Printed in England by Sterling Press

Preface

*T*he British Library has the finest collection of English literary books and manuscripts in the world. Founded in 1753 with three libraries of great breadth and significance, it has acquired further items of national importance ever since. Among these may be counted the unique tenth-century manuscript of the epic Anglo-Saxon poem 'Beowulf'; the Book of Margery Kempe, the earliest known autobiography in the English language, which was discovered in the same year (1934) as the manuscripts of Thomas Malory's 'Le Morte D'Arthur' and Samuel Taylor Coleridge's 'Kubla Khan'; the neatly written copy of Jane Eyre sent to the printer by Charlotte Brontë; two cancelled draft chapters of Jane Austen's Persuasion; and unique and important letters from John Donne, Alexander Pope and Mary Shelley. Spectacular printed works include first editions of William Shakespeare and some of the earliest texts ever published in England, including Geoffrey Chaucer's Canterbury Tales and William Caxton's Confessio Amantis. The Library's modern holdings are no less impressive, either in book or manuscript form, from the early twentieth-century works of Virginia Woolf, T.S. Eliot and Thomas Hardy, to the contemporary writings of Harold Pinter and Andrew Motion.

This short book illustrates, often for the first time, many of the works mentioned above, in addition to other unique collection items. It is published to mark the Library's major literary exhibition, Chapter & Verse: 1000 Years of English Literature. In some ways, both the exhibition and the book may be said to open and close with 'Beowulf'. For in this story, an anonymous Anglo-Saxon master and one of the greatest poets alive today meet to demonstrate the infinite variety not only of literary tradition, but of creative expression itself.

Chris Fletcher, Curator of Literary Manuscripts
The British Library, March 2000

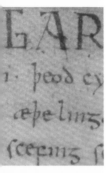

'Beowulf'

Cotton Vitellius A. XV

Some time around the year 1000 an anonymous scribe wrote down the epic Anglo-Saxon poem 'Beowulf'. The author of the poem is not known and it has been suggested that it developed orally from as early on as the seventh-century. Other copies of the poem may have been made but this is the only one known to exist.

The poem tells the story of Beowulf, a fifth- or sixth-century Scandinavian warrior hero, who rids the Danish kingdom of a terrible monster, Grendel, and his vengeful mother. His prowess is rewarded with a gift of lands, which he rules in peace for fifty years. A dragon, revenging the theft of a goblet from its hoard, attacks Beowulf's people and he once again goes into battle. Although the dragon is killed with the help of a loyal subject, Beowulf is mortally wounded. His funeral pyre and a prophecy of disaster for the king-dom provides a magnificent and terrible conclusion to the poem.

'Beowulf' is a complex poem which works on many levels. Most simply, it is a powerful and compelling tale of a great man's battles with monsters. It can also be read, however, as a remarkably perceptive examination of early power politics, an allegorical account of the conflict between early Christian and Pagan religious codes, or as an archetypal example of a story of good versus evil. Well over 1000 years after its composition it continues to be taught in the original Anglo-Saxon as a founding text of the English literary tradition. Perhaps more importantly (and especially when translated by a poet as gifted as Seamus Heaney – see page 46), it is increasingly read for sheer pleasure.

ÞÆT ÞE GARDE

na inȝeardagum. þeod cyninȝa
þrym ȝefrunon huða æþelingaſ elle
fremedon. oft ſcyld ſcefing ſceaþe
þreatum moneȝū mæȝþum meodo ſetl
ofteah eȝſode eorl ſyððan æreſt pearð
fea ſceaft funden he þæſ frofre ȝeba
peox under polcnum peorð myndum þah
oð þ him æȝhpylc þara ymb ſittendra
ofer hron rade hyran ſcolde ȝomban
ȝyldan þþæſ ȝod cyning. ðæm eafera pæſ
æfter cenned ȝeong inȝeardum þone ȝod
ſende folce tofrofre fyren ðearfe on
ȝeat þ hie ærdruȝon aldor leaſe lanȝe
hpile him þæſ lif frea puldreſ pealdend
porold are forȝeaf beopulf pæſ bren

'The Gawain Poet' (fl. c.1380)
Pearl

Cotton Nero A. X, f.42

The author of 'Pearl' remains one of the most mysterious figures in English literature. We know little other than that he was probably attached to a noble house in the North of England in the late fourteenth-century and that his four known poems – including 'Sir Gawain and the Green Knight'- survive only in this manuscript, which includes several illustrations.

The poem describes a father's anger, sorrow and incomprehension at the loss of his infant daughter, or 'Pearl'. Dreaming upon her grave, he sees her on the other side of a river, grown up and radiantly dressed. She reproaches him for his sorrow but, overcome with longing, he plunges in to join her. Although he soon awakes, still a grieving man in the mortal world, he is able to find some consolation in the thought that his daughter is now a 'queen of heaven'. The manuscript here shows the father's amazed reaction on seeing his daughter, a moment translated from the text of the poem by J. R.R. Tolkien:

'O Pearl!' said I, 'in pearls arrayed,
Are you my pearl whose loss I mourn?
Lament alone by night I made,
Much longing I have hid for thee forlorn,
Since to the grass you from me strayed.'

38

42

38

Geoffrey Chaucer (*c*.1343-1400)
The Canterbury Tales

Lansdowne MS 851, f.2

Geoffrey Chaucer, a charismatic and adventurous civil servant, was credited by a friend as being 'the first finder of our fair language'. At a time when most important poetry was written in Anglo-Norman or Latin, his brilliant use of English played a central role in establishing the literary language we recognise today. *The Canterbury Tales*, blending supreme narrative skill with an extraordinary talent for characterisation, is Chaucer's comic masterpiece: every social type is teased in the pilgrimage from Southwark to Canterbury, including the author himself.

Chaucer is the first English writer to have been accurately represented in portraits – although these are extremely rare. This early manuscript copy of *The Canterbury Tales* opens with an illustration of the poet reading. His surprisingly sober expression is more than made up for by his jaunty red socks.

Whan þat Aprill wiþ his schoures soote
þe droughte of march haþe perced to þe roote
And baþed euery veyne in suche lycoure
Of whiche vtue engendrid is þe floure
Whan zephirus eke wiþ his sweete breþe
Inspired haþe in euy holte & heþe
The tendre croppes & þe yonge sonne
haþe in þe rame his half cours ronne
And smal foules maken melodye
þat slepen alnyght wiþ open yhe

So prikkeþ hem nature in hir corages
Than longen folke to gone one pilgrimages
And palmeres for to seke straunge stroudes
To ferne halolwes kowþe in sundry londes
And specially from euy schyres ende
Of Engelond to Canterburi þei wend
The holy blissful martir for to seke
Þat hem haþ holpen whan þei were seke
It befil þan in þat seson vpon a daie
In Suthewerke att þe tabard as I laie
Redi to wende on my pilgremage
To Canterburie wiþ ful deuoute corage
At nyght was come in to þat hostellerie
Wel nyne and twente in a companye
Of sundre folke be aventure yfalle
In felaushipe & Pilgrimes were þei alle
To warde Canterburi þat wolde ride
The chambres & stables weren wyde
And wele weren esede att þe beste
An schortly whan þe son was to reste
So had I spoken wiþ hem euychone
Þat I was of her felawshipe anone
And maade forward erly for to rise
To take owre waie þere as I yow deuise
Bot naþeles while I haue time & space
Er þat I forper in þis tale pace
Me þenkeþ it accordant to resone
To tell yow all þe condicione
Of iche of hem so as it semeþ me
And whiche þei were & of whate degre
And eke in whatte arrue þat þei were inne
And att a knyghte þan wol I furst be gynne.

y goftly fadir y me confeffe
ffirft to god and then to yow
That at a wyndow wot ye how
I ftale a coffe of gret fwetnes
hich don was out avifynes
But hit is doon not vndoon now

y goftly
irft to

ut y reftore it fhall dowtles
Ageyn if fo be that y woll
And that god y make a vow
And ellis y axe foryefnes

y goftly
irft to

Charles d'Orléans (1394-1465)
'My Gostly Fadir'

Harley MS 683, f.88v

Captured at the battle of Agincourt in 1415, the French nobleman Charles D'Orléans was imprisoned in England for twenty-five years. During his incarceration he wrote a series of love lyrics, now in the National Library of France. Of the many manuscripts relating to the sequence, that owned by the British Library is among the most important. Although not literal translations, the majority of the English poems echo the original French. Some commentators see them as the work of an English author, inspired by Charles; others have suggested that they are new versions by Charles himself.

This song, which has no French counterpart, takes the form of a confession made to a priest by a lover who has 'stolen a kiss of great sweetness'. He vows to 'restore' the sin, leaving us – and, presumably, his 'gostly fadir' – wondering whether he truly means to repent or has every intention of returning the kiss to his sweetheart!

My gostly fadir I me confesse   *(My holy father)*
First to god and then to yow

That at a wyndow, wot ye how,   *(you understand how)*
I stale a cosse of great swetnes
Which done was out avisynes   *(without premeditation)*
But hit is doon, not undoon, now

Another late fifteenth-century copy of the sequence includes a magnificent illumination of the Tower of London (reproduced on page 2). Charles is represented several times; most importantly, he can be seen at work on his manuscript, under heavy guard.

11

Schort tretys of a creatur sett in grett pompe &
pride of ye world whech sythen was drawyn to owyr
lord be gret pouerte sekenes schams & gret repreuys
in many dyuers contrees & placys of whech tribulacyon su
schal ben schewed aft not in ordyr as it fellyn but as
ye creatur cowd han mend of hem whan it wer wretyn
ffor it was xx zer & mor fro tym ye creatur had for
sake ye world and besyly clef on to owr lord or yo bok
was wretyn. not wythstondyng yo creatur had greet
cownsel for to don wryten hyr tribulacyons & hyr feling
gs. And a whyte frer pferyd hyr to wryte frely yf sche
wold. And sche was warnyd in hyr spyryt yt sche xuld
not wryte so sone. And many zerys aft sche was bodyn
in hyr spyryt for to wrytyn. And yan zet it was wretyn
fyrst be a man whech cowd neyther wel wryten englysch
ne duch. so it was on able for to be red but only be
specyal grace. for y was so mech obloquie & slawndyr
of yo creatur. yt y wold fewe men beleue yo creatur
And so at y last a prest was sor mevyd for to wrytin
yo tretys & he cowd not wel redyn it of a iiij zer
to gedir & sythen be ye reqst of yo creatur & copel
lyng of hys owyn consciens he asayd agayn for to
rede it & it was mech mor esy. yan it was a for tyme
And so he gan to wryten in ye zer of our lord a.a.
CCCC. xxxbj. on ye day next aftir mary maudelyn
aftir ye informacyon of yo creatur. [Capm I]

han yo creatur was xx zer of age or sumdele
mor sche was maryed to a worschep ful burgeys of ly
and was wth chylde wth in schort tyme as kynde
wold. And aftir yat sche had conceyued sche was labowrd
wyth grett accessys tyl ye chyld was born & yan what
for labor sche had in chyldyng & for seknesse goyng be
forn sche dyspered of hyr lyfe. Wenyng sche mygth not
leuyn. And yan sche sent for hyr gostly fadyr, for sche

Margery Kempe (*c.*1373–*c.*1439)
The Book of Margery Kempe

Add. MS 61823

The earliest surviving autobiography written in the English
language was discovered in 1934, some five hundred years after
its composition, by a man searching for a lost table-tennis ball.
It describes the extraordinary and adventurous life of a Norfolk
woman whose early temptations led her, much to the annoyance
of her husband, to follow a life of devotion, pilgrimage and chastity.

The account was first dictated by Kempe and then written down
by a scribe shortly after her death. Before its remarkable discovery,
all that was known of the work were seven extremely rare pages of
extracts printed by William Caxton's one-time assistant, Wynkyn de
Worde, in 1501.

Robert Burton (1577-1640)
The Anatomy of Melancholy

G. 19650.

'The Author is said to have labour'd long in the Writing of this Book to suppress his own Melancholy, and yet did but improve it … I have heard that nothing could make him laugh, but going down to the Bridge-foot in Oxford and hearing the Barge-men scold and storm and swear at one another, at which he would set his Hands to his Sides, and laugh most profusely.'

According to Bishop Kennett's observation of 1728 (quoted above), *The Anatomy of Melancholy* was apparently prompted by the gloomy disposition of its author, Robert Burton, a bookish man who turned his back on travel, marriage and success. Whatever its personal inspiration, the work provides a strange, compelling and varied study (or 'anatomy') of depressed states of mind, whether in relation to faith, love or even erotic passion. Among the different melancholic images on the title-page is a portrait of the author, under his pseudonym 'Democritus Junior'.

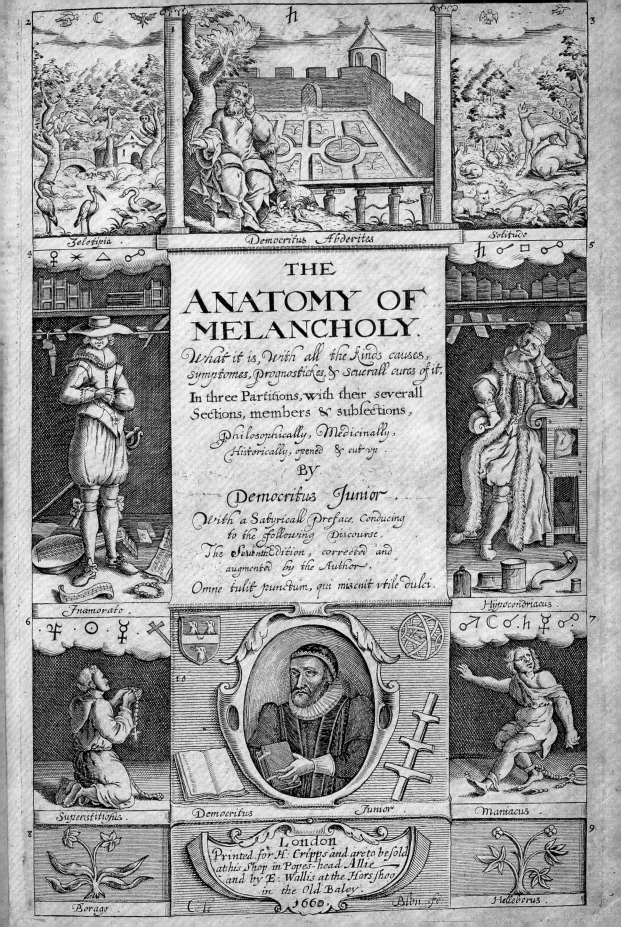

Zelotipia

Democritus Abderites

Solitudo

THE ANATOMY OF MELANCHOLY.

What it is, With all the kinds, causes, symptomes, Prognostickes, & severall cures of it.

In three Partitions, with their severall Sections, members & subsections,

Philosophically, Medicinally, Historically, opened & cut up.

BY

Democritus Junior.

With a Satyricall Preface, Conducing to the following Discourse.

The Seventh Edition, corrected and augmented by the Author.

Omne tulit punctum, qui miscuit utile dulci.

Inamorato.

Hipocondriacus.

Superstitiosus.

Democritus Junior.

Maniacus.

Borago

Helleborus.

London
Printed for H: Cripps and are to be sold at his Shop in Popes-head Allie and by E: Wallis at the Horsshoo in the Old Baley.
1660.

Οτι ουκ εστιν ημιν η παλη προς αιμα και σαρκα, αλλα προς τας αρχας,
προς τας εξεσιας, προς τ8ς κοσμοκρατορας τ8 σκοτ8ς τ8 αιωνος τ8τ8. προς
τα πνευματικα της πονηριας εν τοις επουρανιοις.

ΕΦΕΣ: 5 Κεφ. 12 ver

Vala

Night the First

The Song of the Aged Mother which shook the heavens with wrath
Hearing the march of long resounding strong heroic Verse
Marshalld in order for the day of Intellectual Battle
The heavens quake, the earth was moved & shudderd & the mountains
With all their woods, the streams & valleys: waild in dismal fear

Four Mighty Ones are in every Man; a Perfect Unity
Cannot Exist. but from the Universal Brotherhood of Eden
The Universal Man. To Whom be Glory Evermore Amen

Los was the fourth immortal starry one, & in the Earth
Of a bright Universe. Empery attended day & night
Days & nights of revolving joy, Urthona was his name

John XVII c.

John T c. 14 v
και εσκ̣ρ̣
εν ημ̣

In

William Blake (1757-1827)
The Four Zoas

Add. MS 39764

William Blake, now universally regarded as a genius, found no fame in his lifetime. Trained from the age of fourteen as an engraver, he spent hours sketching monuments in Westminster Abbey where he developed a fascination with the human form and the gothic style. A radical distrust of authority and powerful personal visions – he apparently once saw angels on Peckham Rye – led him to reject a conventional life. Instead, he established himself in Lambeth, south London, designing, engraving, illustrating, writing and printing works in conditions of poverty and under continual suspicion.

The manuscript of 'The Four Zoas', a dense and complex poem, shows an imagination working at white heat as it fuses both literary and artistic inspirations. Blake started the poem after receiving a commission to illustrate Edward Young's poem 'Night Thoughts'. Working on the proofs of another man's work, he perhaps felt inspired to exercise his own unique creative talent.

Samuel Taylor Coleridge (1772-1834)
Kubla Khan

Add. MS 50847, f.1v

'Kubla Khan', one of literature's most famous, discussed and
puzzled-over creations, survives here in one of its most celebrated
and curious manuscripts. At the end of the poem, Coleridge records
the mysterious circumstances of its composition:

*'This fragment with a good deal more, not recoverable, composed, in a
sort of Reverie brought on by two grains of opium, taken to check a
dysentry, at a Farm House between Porlock & Linton, a quarter of a
mile from Culbone Church, in the fall of the year, 1797'*

The account conflicts with the version Coleridge published in
1816, in many details of time, place and circumstance, including
the omission of the famous interruption by the 'person on business
from Porlock'. The actual events leading to and surrounding the
composition of this imaginative masterpiece look likely to remain
forever uncertain.

In Xannadù did Cubla Khan
A stately Pleasure-Dome decree;
Where Alph, the sacred River, ran
Thro' Caverns measureless to Man
Down to a sunless Sea.
So twice six miles of fertile ground
With Walls and Towers were compass'd round:
And here were Gardens bright with sinuous Rills
Where blossom'd many an incense-bearing Tree,
And here were Forests ancient as the Hills
Enfolding sunny Spots of Greenery.
But o! that deep romantic Chasm, that slanted
Down a green Hill athwart a cedarn Cover,
A savage Place, as holy and inchanted
As e'er beneath a waning Moon was haunted
By Woman wailing for her Dæmon Lover.
From forth this Chasm with hideous Turmoil seething,
As if this Earth in fast thick Pants were breathing,
A mighty Fountain momently was forc'd,
Amid whose swift half-intermitted Burst
Huge Fragments vaulted like rebounding Hail,
Or chaffy Grain beneath the Thresher's Flail:
And mid these dancing Rocks at once & ever
It flung up momently the sacred River.
Five miles meandring with a mazy Motion
Thro' Wood and Dale the sacred River ran,
Then reach'd the Caverns measureless to Man
And sank in Tumult to a lifeless Ocean;
And mid this Tumult Cubla heard from far
Ancestral Voices prophesying War.
　　The Shadow of the Dome of Pleasure
　　Floated midway on the Wave
　　Where was heard the mingled Measure
　　From the Fountain and the Cave
It was a miracle of rare Device

William Wordsworth (1770–1850)

I Wandered Lonely as a Cloud

Add. MS 47864, f.80

This poem by William Wordsworth is one of the best known in the English language. It comes from the highly important manuscript volume used in the publication of *Poems, in Two Volumes* (1807).

The printer is here instructed to include the poem in a section entitled 'Moods of my own mind' – yet such a claim to uniqueness of inspiration is perhaps challenged by imagery which strongly evokes his beloved sister Dorothy's own descriptions of daffodils, which 'tossed and reeled and danced'. The manuscript was written out on Wordsworth's behalf by his wife Mary, who makes an intriguing false start.

To the Printer

after the Poem (in the set under the title
of "Moods of my own mind") beginning
"The Cock is crowing" please to insert
the two following properly number'd & number
the succeeding ones accordingly

~~I wandered like a lonely~~

I wandered lonely as a Cloud
That floats on high oer Vales and Hills,
When all at once I saw a crowd
A host of dancing Daffodils;
Along the Lake beneath the trees
Ten thousand dancing in the breeze.

The Waves beside them danced, but they
Outdid the sparkling Waves in glee:—
A Poet could not but be gay
In such a laughing company:
I gaz'd—and gaz'd—but little thought
What wealth the shew to me had brought.

For oft when on my couch I lie
In vacant or in pensive mood,
They flash upon that inward eye
Which is the bliss of solitude
And then my heart with pleasure fills,
And dances with the Daffodils.

Chapter 11

~~Who can be in doubt~~ ~~of~~

~~ston?~~ Who can be in doubt of
what followed? When any two
young People take it into their
heads to marry, they are pretty sure
by perseverance to ~~carry their point~~ ~~gain~~ ~~their~~
~~opposition~~ be they ever so poor,
or ever so imprudent, or ever so
little likely to be necessary to each
other's ultimate comfort. This may
be bad Morality to conclude with,
but I believe it to be Truth —
and if such practises succeed, how
should a Capt. W— & an Emma to
fail, with the advantage of Maturity
of Mind, consciousness of Right, &
an Independant Fortune between
them — ~~they~~ of bearing down every oppo-
sition? They might in fact, have
borne down a great deal more
than they met with, for there
was little to distress them beyond
the want of Graciousness & Warmth.
Mr W— made no objection, & Eliz: ~~did~~
did nothing worse than look cold
& unconcerned. — Capt. W— with
£25,000 — & as high in Air

Jane Austen (1775-1817)
Persuasion

Egerton MS 3038, f.9v

Jane Austen's subtle portrayals of human behaviour in shrewdly
observed social situations has made her one of the most widely read
novelists in the English language. Ironically enough, in her own day
her works met with little popularity.

Persuasion was Austen's last novel, begun in 1815 and published
posthumously in 1818. Although written when her health was
failing, it is generally regarded to be as skilful and profound as any
of her earlier achievements. Two final chapters of the novel survive
in manuscript. Austen, in fact, revised the novel's conclusion, giving
her heroine, Anne Elliot, a much stronger role in prompting
Wentworth's declaration of love.

John Keats (1795-1821)

Hyperion

Add. MS 37000, f.1

This 'epic fragment' was begun in late 1818 in Hampstead and published in 1820, just one year before its young author died of tuberculosis in Rome. 'Hyperion' describes war among the ancient gods, with the old order of Titans finally deposed by Apollo, god of poetry and music. As so often in Keats's work, the subject seems to symbolise the poet's own struggle for fresh inspiration.

Keats, who trained as a doctor before turning to poetry, never enjoyed literary success in his lifetime; his sadly ironic belief that his work would remain unread after his death is reflected in the words he chose for his grave in Rome: 'here lies one whose name is writ in water'.

Deep in the shady sadness of a Vale,
Far sunken from the healthy breath of Morn,
Far from the fiery noon, and ~~evening~~ Eve's one star,
Sat grey hair'd Saturn quiet as a Stone,
Still as the Silence round about his Lair.
Forest on forest hung above his head
~~Like Clouds that whose besom Thundrous bosoms~~
Like Cloud on Cloud. No stir of air was there,
~~Not so much life as what an evening robin~~
~~Would spread upon a field of green said corn:~~
But where the dead leaf fell, there did it rest.
A Stream went voiceless by, still deadened more
By reason of his fallen divinity
~~Spreading acriff it~~
Spreading a shade: the Naiad mid her reds
Press'd her cold finger closer to her lips.

Along the margin sand large foot marks went
No further than to where his feet had stay'd,
And slept ~~without~~ there since ~~a motion; since that time~~ where the ground
His old right hand lay nerveless ~~on the ground~~ listless, dead
Unsceptered; and his ~~white browd~~ realmless eyes were closd;
While his ~~bowd~~ bow'd head seem'd listening to the Earth
His Ancient Mother for some comfort yet.

Thus the old Eagle drowsy with ~~his grief~~ great ~~neff~~ grief
Sat moulting his weak Plumage never more
To be restored or soar against the Sun,
While his three Sons upon Olympus stood —
It seem'd no force could wake him from his place

* Not so much like as on a Summers day
Robs not at all the dandelion's fleece

Charlotte Brontë (1816-1855)
Jane Eyre
Add. MS 43475, f.179

This is Charlotte Brontë's handwritten manuscript of *Jane Eyre*, open at Rochester's proposal – perhaps the most celebrated in fiction. The manuscript was sent by Charlotte to her printer in August 1847 after she had written the novel at great speed, spurred on by the publication successes enjoyed that year by her sisters, Emily and Anne, and undaunted by the rejection of her first novel, 'The Professor'. It appeared in print just two months later and met with great acclaim, fully answering her publisher's demands for a story of 'thrilling excitement'.

The manuscript – one of three volumes – is remarkably neat, given the speed with which Brontë worked, and has few corrections. It provides a wonderful example of what Elizabeth Gaskell described as her 'clear, legible, delicate traced writing'.

His face was very much agitated and very much flushed, and there were strong workings in the features and strange gleams in the eyes.

"Oh Jane, you torture me!" he exclaimed "With that searching and yet faithful and generous look – you torture me!"

"How can I do that? If you are true and your offer real, my only feeling to you must be gratitude and devotion – that cannot torture."

"Gratitude!" he ejaculated, and added wildly "Jane accept me quickly – say, Edward, give me my name, Edward, I will marry you."

"Are you in earnest? Do you truly love me? Do you sincerely wish me to, be your wife ~~marry you~~?"

"I do – and if an oath is necessary to satisfy you – I swear it."

"Then Sir – I will marry you."

"Edward – my little wife!"

"Dear Edward!"

"Come to me – come to me entirely now." said he, and added in his deepest tone, speaking in my ear as his cheek was laid on mine, "Make my happiness – I will make yours."

"God, pardon me!" he subjoined erelong "And man, meddle not with me; I have her and will hold her."

"There is no one to meddle Sir; I have no kindred to interfere."

"No – that is the best of it." he said and if I had loved him less

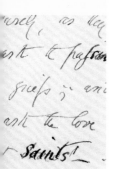

Elizabeth Barrett Browning (1806-1861)
Sonnets from the Portugese

Add. MS 43487, f.49

Shown here is one of English Literature's most famous love poems,
written during one of its most famous love affairs. The poem is the
penultimate in the celebrated sequence which movingly describes the
gradual intensification and flowering of Elizabeth Barrett's feelings
for fellow-poet Robert Browning, with whom she would secretly
elope to Italy. Underneath the last sonnet Elizabeth has written
'Married – September 12th/1846', but it was not until 1849, after
the birth of their son, that Robert first learned of the remarkable
manuscript written by the woman he fondly nicknamed 'my little
Portugese'.

The small notebook was treasured by Robert Browning after Elizabeth's
death in 1861. When Browning died in 1889 it passed to his son and
was finally acquired by the British Museum in 1933.

How do I love thee? Let me count the ways!—
I love thee to the depth & breadth & height
My soul can reach, when feeling out of sight
For the ends of Being and Ideal Grace.
I love thee to the level of everyday's
Most quiet need, by sun & candlelight—
I love thee freely, as men strive for Right;—
I love thee purely, as they turn from Praise:;
I love thee with the passion put to use
In my old griefs;; and with my childhood's faith.
I love thee with the love I seemed to lose
With my lost Saints!— I love thee with the breath,
Smiles, tears, of all my life!— and, if God choose,
I shall but love thee better after death.

'Lewis Carroll' (1832-1898)
(Charles Lutwidge Dodgson)
Alice's Adventures
Under Ground

Add. MS 46700, ff. 19v–20

On 4 July 1862, the Reverend Charles Dodgson, a young mathematics tutor at Christ Church, Oxford, entertained three little girls on a river trip with an extraordinary and fantastic 'fairy tale' which was to become one of the most famous children's stories of all time. Alice Liddell, its ten-year-old heroine, begged him to write it out for her, but had to wait two years until she received this beautifully hand-written little volume, with Dodgson's own charming illustrations, entitled 'Alice's Adventures Under Ground'.

In 1866 Dodgson published a revised and expanded version, *Alice's Adventures in Wonderland*, under the pseudonym 'Lewis Carroll'. The manuscript remained with Alice for many years, until financial difficulties compelled her to sell it at auction in 1928. It was purchased by an American collector but eventually returned to Britain in 1946.

The page shown here contains one of Dodgson's illustrations of Alice after she has drunk from the 'little magic bottle' found in the White Rabbit's house.

half the bottle, she found her head pressing against the ceiling, and she stooped to save her neck from being broken, and hastily put down the bottle, saying to herself "that's quite enough— I hope I sha'n't grow any more— I wish I hadn't drunk so much!"

Alas! it was too late: she went on growing and growing, and very soon had to kneel down: in another minute there was not room even for this, and she tried the effect of lying down, with one elbow against the door, and the other arm curled round her head. Still she went on growing, and as a last resource she put one arm out of the window, and one foot up the chimney, and said to herself "now I can do no more — what will become of me?"

Rudyard Kipling (1865-1936)
Just So Stories

Add. MS 59840, f.33

Kipling's 'Just So Stories' are loved by children and adults alike.
Shown here is the manuscript volume sent to the printer for
publication in 1902; it clearly demonstrates how Kipling's skill
as a writer was matched by his superb artistic ability.

This is his illustration to the story of 'The Elephant's Child', which
tells how a baby elephant of 'insatiable curiosity', for which he was
frequently spanked, acquired his trunk. Kipling describes the picture
earlier in the manuscript:

*'This is the Elephant's Child having his nose pulled by the crocodile.
He is much surprised and astonished and hurt, and he is talking through
his nose and saying 'Led go! You are hurtig be!' He is pulling very hard,
and so is the Crocodile; but the Bi-Coloured-Python-Rock-Snake is
hurrying through the water to help the Elephant's Child ...'*

Included among the other famous stories in this manuscript are
'How the Camel got his Hump' and 'The Cat that Walked by
Himself'.

Sir Arthur Conan Doyle (1859-1930)
The Adventure of the Missing Three Quarter

Add. MS 50065, f.2

Of all literary characters who have taken on a life of their own, Sherlock Holmes is perhaps the most famous. Sir Arthur Conan Doyle first breathed life into him in 1887, only to kill him off at the Reichenbach Falls in 1893. Public outcry, however, forced the author to resurrect him eight years later in *The Hound of the Baskervilles*, and he went on to survive another thirty-five stories.

In this adventure, written in about 1904, Dr Watson's narrative soon turns to a worried consideration of his master's dangerous tendency to addictive substances:

'Now I knew that under ordinary conditions he no longer craved for this artificial stimulus but I was aware the fiend was not dead but sleeping.'

The manuscript was presented to the British nation on 22 May 1959 to mark the one-hundredth anniversary of the birth of Sir Arthur Conan Doyle by a group of American well-wishers, together with the Friends of the National Libraries and the Sherlock Holmes Society of London.

The Adventure of the Missing Three Quarter.

We were fairly accustomed to receive weird telegrams at Baker
Street but I ~~can remember~~ have a particular recollection of one which reached us on a gloomy February
morning some seven or eight years ago and gave Mr Sherlock Holmes
a puzzled quarter of an hour. It was addressed to him and ran
thus

"Please await me, Terrible misfortune, ~~uncertain how~~
~~to act~~. Right wing three quarter, ~~indispensable~~ missing. indispensible
tomorrow. Overton"

"Strand post mark and dispatched 9.36" said
Holmes, reading it over and over. "Mr Overton was evidently
considerably excited when he ~~dispatched~~ sent it and some what
incoherent in consequence. Well, well, he will be here I dare say ~~by~~ by
~~the time that the table is cleared~~ the time I have looked through the Times and then we shall know all about
it. Even the most insignificant problem would be welcome in these
stagnant times."

Things had indeed been very slow with us, and I
had learned to dread such periods of inaction for I knew by
experience that my companion's brain was so abnormally active
that it was dangerous to leave it without material upon which to
work. For years I had gradually weaned him from that drug
mania which had threatened once to ~~destroy~~ check his remarkable
career nature. Now I knew that under ordinary conditions he no longer
craved for this artificial stimulus but I was well aware that the
fiend was not dead but sleeping, and I have known that the
sleep was a light one and the waking near when in periods of
idleness I have seen the drawn look upon Holmes' ascetic face,
and the brooding of his deep set and inscrutable eyes. Therefore
I blessed Mr Overton, whoever he might be, since he had come
with his enigmatic message to break that dangerous calm which
brought more peril danger to my friend than all the storms of his
tempestuous life.

Adlestrop

Yes, I remember Adlestrop —
At least the name ~~One afternoon~~
Of heat ~~the express train~~ ~~struck~~ drew up there
~~against its custom~~. It 'twas June.

The steam hissed. Someone cleared his throat.
No one left & no one came
On the bare platform. What I saw
Was Adlestrop. only the name,

And, willows, willow-herb & grass,
And meadowsweet. The hay cocks dry
Were not less still & lonely fair
Than the high cloud~~lets~~ in the sky.

And all that minute a blackbird sang
Close by, and round him, mistier,
Farther & farther, all the birds
Of Oxfordshire & Gloucestershire.

Yes, I remember Adlestrop
The name, because
~~......~~. One aftern[oon]
Of heat, the express train drew
~~......~~
Unwontedly. It was late Jun[e]

Edward Thomas (1878-1917)
Adlestrop

Add. MS 44990, f.10v

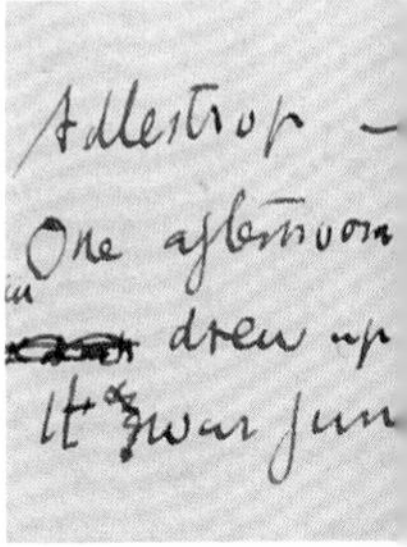

Just before the First World War a railway train carrying Edward
Thomas stopped briefly at the Cotswold station of Adlestrop, an
event which inspired one of the best loved of English poems. The
beguiling simplicity of the language and intense observation of
detail somehow create in the poem an atmosphere both mysterious
and elegiac, transforming a commonplace event into something
marvellous. A draft of the poem, dating from 8 January 1915, is
shown here in a manuscript volume later presented to the British
Museum by the poet's wife Helen.

Edward Thomas was born in Lambeth, south London, in 1878
and educated at Oxford where he married Helen Noble. Scraping
a living as a journalist and jobbing writer, he began writing poetry
in 1914. On 14 July 1915 he enlisted in the Artists' Rifles and on
9 April 1917 he was killed at the opening of the Battle of Arras.

Wilfred Owen (1893-1918)
Anthem for Dead Youth

Add. MS 43721, f.55

Just one week before the end of the First World War, Wilfred Owen
was killed in action, leaving behind a remarkable and moving
collection of poems. Above all else, the poet hoped to shock English
readers into an awareness of the horror and futility of conflict.
'Anthem for Doomed Youth', as it became known, was composed
in the summer of 1917 at Craiglockhart hospital, Edinburgh, where
the poet was sent to recover from shell shock; its title was suggested
by his friend Siegfried Sassoon, who described the work as 'a
revelation'. Owen saw just four poems printed in his lifetime but,
shortly before his death, had started to prepare a complete volume
for publication. His wish was carried through by Sassoon, in an
edition of 1920.

The two volumes of manuscript poems were presented to the
British nation by the Friends of the National Libraries and
various subscribers in 1934.

Anthem for Dead Youth.

What passing-bells for you who die in herds?
  — Only the monstrous anger of ~~more~~ the guns!
  — Only the stuttering rifles' rattled words
Can patter out your hasty orisons.
No chants for you, nor balms, nor wreaths, nor bells,
    Nor any voice of mourning, save the choirs,
~~The~~ And ~~shrill~~ long-drawn ~~demented choirs~~ sighs of wailing shells;
    And bugles calling for you from sad shires.

What candles may we hold to speed you all?
    Not in the hands of boys, but in their eyes
~~Shall~~ Shall shine the holy lights ~~and gleams your~~ of ~~long~~ goodbyes.
The pallor of girls' brows ~~shall~~ may be your pall; comrade
Your flowers, the tenderness of ~~pale~~ ~~mortal~~ minds,
And each slow dusk, a drawing-down of blinds.

               Wilfred Owen.

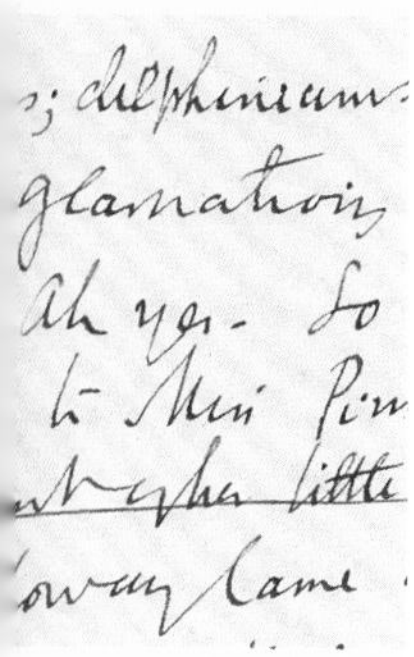

Virginia Woolf (1882-1941)
Mrs Dalloway

Add. MS 51045, f.136

Mrs Dalloway traces the thoughts, memories and emotions of
one character through the course of a single day in London.
The novel's inventive narrative technique is brilliantly assured,
its evocation of isolation and loneliness moving and beautiful.
Indeed, it is hard at times not to associate the heroine's sadness
with that of Woolf herself, who suffered mental anguish
throughout a life which she eventually ended in 1941. The
novel, originally entitled 'The Hours', was published in 1925,
helping to establish Woolf as an important exponent of the
Modernist style.

One manuscript volume of three is illustrated here, showing
a wonderful litany of flower names in the author's favoured
purple ink.

by the red faced, button faced Miss Pym, whose hands were
always bright red, as if they had been stood in cold water with the
flowers where she kept her
flowers.

There were flowers; delphiniums, sweet peas; bunches of lilac;
& carnations, masses of carnations. There were roses; there
were irises & lilies. Ah yes - so she breathed in the earthy
garden smell; talking to Miss Pim, who owed her help, & would
therefore always come ~ the little boy; & come at the box
always when Mrs Dalloway came in, & they let her kind for
kind she had been, years ago; kind she still was, standing there,
looking older, now this year, turning her head, from side to
side among the irises & roses, & nodding tufts of lilac, with
her eyes half closed, snuffing in the delicious scent. And then,
opening her eyes, how fresh, like frilled linen clean from a
laundry laid in wicker trays they looked; & dark &
prim, the red carnations, holding their heads up; ~
& all the sweet peas spreading in their bowls, tinged
violet, snow white, pale, - as if it were the evening, ~
girls in muslin frocks came out to pick sweet peas &
roses after the superb summers day, with its
almost blue-black sky, its delphiniums, its carnations,
its arum lilies, was over; ~ it was the awkward moment
between six & seven, when every flower - roses,
carnations, irises, lilac, glows; white, violet, red, deep orange; every
flower seems to burn by itself, softly, purely
intensely, with magic fire ~ in the misty beds, -
how she loved the grey white moths spinning over
the purple cherry pie, the yellow evening primroses!
        Don't you get fearfully tired, she said
to Miss Pim. Were standing all day
        When do you get your holiday?

Philip Larkin (1922-1985)
Wedding-Wind

Add. MS 52619, f.50

Although by his death in 1985 Larkin had published just four slim
collections of verse, his superb control of tone, technical brilliance
and ability to speak of both the mundane and the marvellous
endeared him to a broad audience. Written when he was just
twenty-four, 'Wedding-Wind' carries several of the poet's unmistak-
able hallmarks: the convincingly intimate voice of the narrator as
she wavers between melancholy and joy; the elemental imagery
contrasted with domestic detail; the shift from the palpable contexts
of the first lines to the metaphysical questionings of the last.

The manuscript reveals much about the process of composition.
A relative lack of amendments in the first verse suggests that the
author got off to a flying start. The heavily reworked second,
however, reflects the extra formal and intellectual demands made
of the poet in his attempt to to carry off a series of complicated
final metaphors.

Larkin's entire working life was spent as a librarian, latterly at the
University of Hull. He was dedicated to retaining modern literary
manuscripts in British institutions and presented this notebook to
the nation in 1963.

The wind blew all my wedding-day
And my wedding-night was the night of the high wind,
And a stable door was banging, again and again,
~~So~~ That he must go and shut it, leaving me
Stupid in candlelight, hearing ~~the~~ rain,
Seeing my face ~~twisted~~ in the ~~brass~~ twisted candlestick,
Yet seeing nothing. When he came back
He said the horses were restless, and I was sad
That any man or beast that night should lack
The happiness I had.

All's travelled ~~settled~~ under the sun ~~with~~ the ~~————~~ Now in the morning wind's blowing.
He has gone to look at the floods ~~fences~~, and I
Carry a chipped pail to the chicken-run,
~~————~~ Set it down, and stare. All is the wind
Hunting through clouds and forests, thrashing
My apron and the hanging clothes on the line ~~————~~.
Can it be borne, this bodying-forth by wind
of joy ~~my~~ each in turn on, ~~like a swinging thread~~
~~the undreamed joy at the root of day and night,~~
Carrying ~~abroad~~? Shall I be let to sleep.
Now this ~~With this~~ perpetual morning shares fills my bed?
~~Will town death conclude~~
~~This~~ Our Kneeling like cattle among new ~~waters of forth~~?
Can
~~Will~~ even death dry up
These new delighted lakes, conclude
Our kneeling as cattle ~~among~~ by all generous waters?

                                                                25 Sep

Canto

P. G. Wodehouse (1881-1975)
Galahad at Blandings

Add. MS 52774, f.95

In 1903 P.G. Wodehouse gave up working as a bank clerk in order
to pursue his literary ambitions. His life was as eventful as it was
controversial. During the Second World War he was captured in
France by the Germans. Imprisoned at first, he was later released on
condition that he remained in Germany. A number of subsequent
broadcasts from Berlin about his captivity provoked accusations of
fascist sympathies. After the war he settled in America, working for
Hollywood and producing numerous stories. He gained American
citizenship in 1955 and was awarded a knighthood just weeks
before his death.

Perhaps most famous for the characters Jeeves and Wooster (who
first appeared in 1917), Wodehouse's inimitable comic flair is
instantly recognisable in a manuscript relating to the novel of
1965, *Galahad at Blandings*. Wodehouse's extraordinary planning
technique – consisting of a critical dialogue with himself – is
revealed here.

*Bring on Lady H with Vee and have Lady H give her
instructions. ('Yes, mum-mee'). Gally — & drive off
and Lady H tells heroine to the v. firm with Ld E. He
will try to sneak away to that pig of his, and you must
stop him.*

August 4.1963

SCENARIO *x This version cuts Cedric out of story*
— unless he takes place of hero X's kid.

1. Tipton, Cedric *x* and Lord Emsworth in New York. (See July 19)

2. Gally and Heroine at Blandings. Gally off to London to meet
Lord E. (See July 19). Hero to go to Emsworth Arms.

3. Next day. Gally and Lord E in train. *Car* Gally tells him Wedges, Cedric,
secretary are at castle. 'Is that tall halfwitted girl with them?' 'No,
she's in London buying clothes, if you mean your niece Veronica. But
a Mrs X and her son are there. I believe you used to know her as Cissie
A.' Plant that Mrs X was a flame of Lord E's twenty-five years ago. He
says he looks forward to meeting her again.

4. They have taken an early train, so get to castle early in afternoon.
Lord E meets Mrs X and asks her if she has seen the Empress. She says
no, and he takes her with kid to sty. There she disillusions him by
saying 'What a revolting animal'. Kid says pig is too fat and needs
exercise. Show Wellbeloved *Simmons* listening and disapproving. *x*

5. Ld E goes back to house, all set for a good read of Whipple and
meets heroine, who says there is an enormous mass of correspondence
for him to answer. She says she is sorting it out and returns to
small room off library to do so. Ld E feels he is up against a
secretary even more of a pest than Baxter.
    Gally comes in and Ld E complains abt heroine. Gally says She is
the least of your troubles. How did you get on with Mrs X? — Ld E
says he can't think what he ever saw in her. — Gally says that after
Ld E left for the sty Colonel Wedge confided in him that Lady Hermione
has told him she is going to try to arrange a marriage between Lord E
and Mrs X. Gally warns him never to be alone with her. If she suggests
a saunter in the rose garden, kick her in the pants'.
    Gally exits, leaving Lord E despondent and apprehensive.

End of First Spasm

6. Show Hero at Emsworth Arms. He is finding life dull and goes to
library to get a book. Sees heroine there. (There is nothing much
to read at castle, unless you are fond of pigs and eithteenth century
sermons). He tries to talk to her but she legs it.
    x See note of Aug 4
    No, this is wrong. See notes of July 24. Beach ought to start
this section, seeing hero in bar and thinking him sinister, it having
been planted that hero has a twisted ear from boxing.
    Then I think hero should go to library and see heroine.
    x Probably the solution wd be to have hero stay not at the Emsworth
Arms but at the inn at Blandings Parva, which can be assumed to be
practically next door to the castle. The trouble abt putting him at
Ems Arms is that it is two miles from castle, so he couldn't follow heroine
without overtaking her. *x*
    What I want is for there to be a library and sweet shop to which
both hero and heroine go.
    In 2 hero asks G if there isn't any place nearer castle than Ems Arms.

Seamus Heaney (1939-)
'Beowulf'

Deposit 9896

It has been said of Seamus Heaney that he 'is the one living poet who can rightly claim to be the Beowulf Poet's heir'. Some 1000 years after the original poem was set down in manuscript (see page 4), the brilliance of his translation was recognised in January 2000 when he won the Whitbread Book Award. Heaney's poem faithfully captures all the power and subtlety of the original, while enriching – often clarifying – its meanings in a vernacular drawn from his own deeply-rooted Irish 'word hoard'.

This page shows Heaney's first attempt to translate 'Beowulf' from the Anglo-Saxon text. Dating from 1980, it was abandoned after only a few lines. Fifteen years later, the poet took up his task again at Glanmore, a spot which had already inspired a famous and much-loved sequence of sonnets. This first and the many subsequent drafts of the opening of the translation show the poet to be a tireless and careful crafter of his work. Heaney hones his typewritten text with annotations, corrections, deletions and revisions, all marked in a vigorous and emphatic hand.

So. The Spear Danes held sway once.

The kings of that clan are fabulous now   *heroes to us*

because of their baravery. ~~They are out~~ heroest us,
                                    we have heard of their feats.

There was Scyld Scefing, the scourge of many tribes,

a wrecker of mead benches, marauding among ~~enemies~~ *foemen*
                       his brothers
This hammer of the ~~Heruli~~ had come far.   *This terror of*
               his foes   *the earl-troops*
He had been a foundlilng but that was forgotten   *had won far*

as his powers waxed and his worth was proved.
in the end
~~A time came when~~ each sept on the neighbouring coasts
                      bowed down and obeyed
beyond the whale-road ~~bent in obedience to him~~
                        him :
and paid (him) (tribute) He was a good king.

After that a son was born to Scyld,

a young cub in the yard, God's gift

to that nation. He knew what they had gone through,

the long times and toubles they had tholed

without a leader; and so the Lord of Life,

the glorious Almighty, made this one renowned.

The son's fame spread far and wide

all through the north. His name was Beowulf.

Scyld had fathered a famous son:

Beowulf's name was known all through the north.   *his*
And that is how a young man should manage for good :
~~A young man should manage for good that way,~~   *gis not a free held*
                                                             while his
he should fend and give freely while his father lives   *father*
                                in age when
so that afterwards ~~when he~~ is ~~old~~ and fighting starts
                                              him
his steadfast companions will stand by ~~their leader~~
and bear the brunt; ~~for~~ to be well spoken of
~~is~~ a ~~man's~~ path to power among people everywhere.

with their leader :

sh And that is how a young man should   good deeds
                                walks his own
                            choose grow by
                                manage his good

Exhibition Acknowledgements

Thanks to all colleagues who have helped with this exhibition, in particular: Helen O'Riain (Children's section), Sally Brown and Elizabeth James (responsible for sections on Hardy, Austen, Barrie, Carroll, Dickens), Hilton Kelliher, Ann Payne, Richard Price, Mervyn Jannetta, Claire Breay, Richard Goulden, Andrew Prescott, Michelle Brown, Justin Clegg, Jacqui Hunt, Greg Buzwell, Janet Benoy, Alan Sterenberg, Geraldine Kenny, Toby Oakes, Anne Rose, Frances Ash-Glover, Kumiko Matsuoka, Cyril Titus, David French, David Way, Kathleen Houghton, Laurence Pordes, Malcolm Smith, Karen Brookfield, Valerie McBurney, Ken Shirreffs, Greg Hayman, Anne Young, Alison Pavier, Alice Prochaska, Colin Wight, Kate Barnes.

Grateful thanks to the following, for loans and other permissions: John Murray, The Brotherton Library, Eton College, Dulwich College, Ashmolean Museum, The Folio Society, Roy Davids, Seamus Heaney, Beryl Bainbridge, P.D. James, Hanif Kureishi, Andrew Motion, Kenneth Baker, Harold Pinter, Simon Armitage, The Royal Literary Fund, and private collectors who wish to remain anonymous.

Thanks are due to Pearson, Axiom Design, Anna Arthur PR.